Poems by
ROBERT NICHOLS

Address to the Smaller Animals

Prints by
Lucia Vernarelli

Harbor Mountain Press
Brownsville, Vermont

Harbor Mountain Press acknowledges the support of
Pentangle Council on the Arts (Woodstock, Vermont)
for this and other literary projects.

*The original version of this book was published in 1976 by Penny Each Press.
Harbor Mountain Press gratefully acknowledges the right to publish this facsimile.*

First Harbor Mountain Press edition 2008

ISBN 0-9786009-3-2

Series Editor:
Peter Money

Production editing:
Barbara Jones

Illustrations:
Lucia Vernarelli

Harbor Mountain Press
Brownsville, Vermont
0 5 0 3 7
www.harbormountainpress.com

Note To The Reader

The re-publishing of this book was embraced by one of the most activistic voices of the 20th century, Robert Nichols' wife Grace Paley. At one of her last readings she read Nichols' poem "The Man Who Sold Mahatma Gandhi Life Insurance." The poem is vintage Robert Nichols—wry, a little lambasting, and endearing. The great pacifist Gandhi takes the insurance, as the title suggests, and remarks in the poem that the American insurance salesman, "sweet-talked me." The Gandhi in the poem was either exhibiting his generosity to all human beings, or, the poet shows that even (especially) the good-hearted can be "had." It is this kind of speech that in the 1960s gave poets and playwrights (Nichols being both) the ability to be funny and dead serious at the same time.

But in this age could it be that poetry itself has been sweet-talked, as have wide portions of an inert populace? "[T]he Angel of Silence stuffs his fist into your mouth" proclaims Nichols' poem "The Four Stages." If pacifism does need "life insurance," it's just as likely protest requires new life, sharper eyes, revived consciousness.

Originally published in 1976 but written over the '60s, Nichols' poems' detail and clamor will serve readers today as a historical measure—and as instructional.

Lucia Vernarelli's images surround Robert Nichols' poems as tender meditations, their shadows highlighting what's left of the personal and the mundane, the tranquil and the deceiving. And through them, no matter what voice the centuries' babel takes "while [we] go stumbling and stumbling through the dark" as Nichols writes: "we do not rest but weep—through the dark, or through the lovely." But then go, laugh, speak. Ring the bell!

—PM

Harbor Mountain Press

Table of Contents

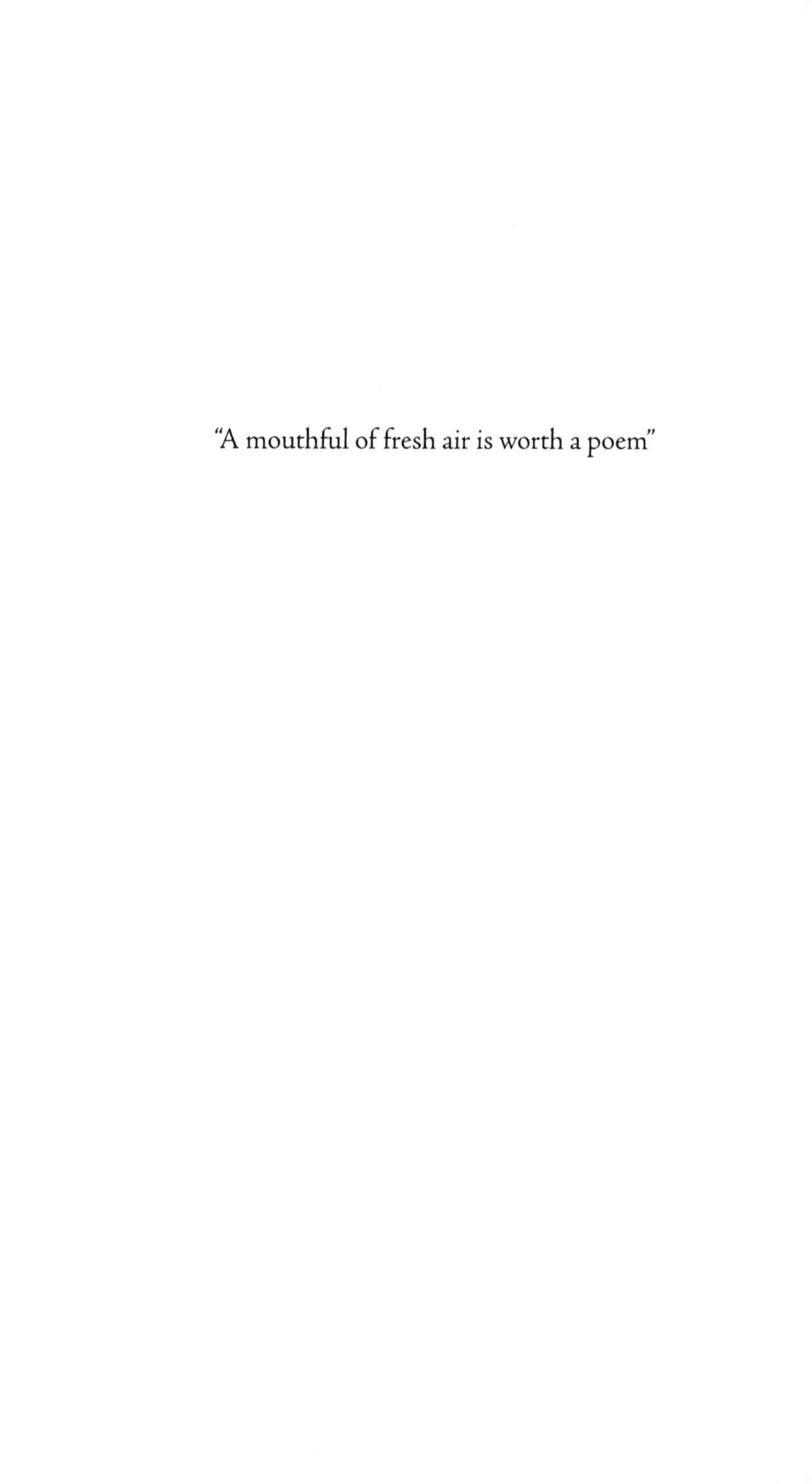

"A mouthful of fresh air is worth a poem"

Foreword

Some of these poems were read out by Bob Nichols at the Deux Meggots coffee house in New York City's Lower East Side, gathering place of poets in the early 1960s. Some were recited or rather shouted out in the air on the Gansvort Street pier jutting out into the Hudson River. Thus ended the decorous literary age of T.S. Eliot and words confined to the printed page. It was the time of turbulent political activity and radicalism as can be seen in the poems honoring Franz Fanon and Bahkunin. Yet there was always about Nichols something of his New England resolutely upper middle class Brahmin heritage: there is a photo of him in the collection *The Beat Scene* in tweed overcoat with velvet collar.

At the time of writing, Bob, with his wife and children, spent some time at the family place in rural Vermont. Hence the "City Haiku / Winter in the park," "Eye Against Consolidated Edison," the first city snow are balanced against the "Country Haiku":

> Everywhere the grass
> Drinks up the night dew
> As the little girl listens to stories

There are poems on woodchucks and hunting wildflowers, poems to each of the three children. Some of these are wry poems and characteristically reveal Nichols' self doubt. There are the bird songs which ring joy.

> But of my own children's cries
>
> which is the sweetest to me now
> and which is the most bitter?

And for Kerstin:

> She has her hand in mine   Will she hate me then
> When I'm old   and the leaves are cold
> on the tree   and she and I
> are no longer green?

There are also some wonderful love poems:

> My love's body at noon
> has closed with wine

But to whom?

And the long poem "Ragas to Ahma" . . . and some family poems, "My Father-In-Me" and "A Cannuck Matriarch," about Bob's grandmother who emigrated from French Canada.

The illustrations for these poems, the prints, are by Lucia Vernarelli, an artist and dear friend of Bob's and myself. . . . Among other things Lucia made handsome posters during the Vietnam war and was with us and many other writers, painters and musicians in the movement—Angry Arts.

I knew Bob's poems before I knew him. It was then important that I get to know the maker of the poems who I soon began to love.

—Grace Paley

Poems by
ROBERT NICHOLS

Address to the Smaller Animals

Prints by
Lucia Vernarelli

ADDRESS TO THE SMALLER ANIMALS

I pitch through the dark   a heavy-footed animal
Smaller animals take cover   I'm coming
through the dark rift of the sky and through the pines

All animals smaller than me   I'm coming
Weasel I'm coming   Woodchuck I'm coming
Mole smaller than me   Porcupine smaller than me
                              Fieldmouse smaller than me

Snake slide into your hole
Rustle your cold scales over the rock   snake
                    listen to me
                    on the rock next to you   as you move fast
liquifying and condensing your dark links

Worm do the same thing   you are a slitherer also
Spider do the same thing   feel my sound in the tree next to you
screw up your bridges of spit into you   spider
Chipmunk   someone is coming who is larger than owl
Night-flitting bat someone is on his way
                    who is greater than owl

As I walk through the wood heavily
Rabbit bounds off a little way
                    and stops and looks back
Deer bounds off a little way and looks back
                    arching his neck
Partridge looks back
Curious to see me who am no different from
                              Everyman?

Why these animals all have the loveliest eyes!

            While I go stumbling and stumbling through the dark
brothers   under the dark stream of the sky
                    between the black dykes of the pines
the sky condenses and rarefies over my head

WHERE IS BERTHOLD BRECHT'S LAST CIGAR?

Gnostic Poem

I don't know the names of the trees
I don't know West Wind's name
I don't know the springs under the lake/
                where do they come from?   are they cool?

They say a stream ran underground once to cool itself
     and found Persephone in hell   /sucking barley sugar/
                      is this true?

When do pickerel bite? He told me it was when
     mayflies come/   which is when apple opens
        Where do these three things winter:
        the fish/   the fly/   and the bud?

Is there another city   under the City of Paris?
as there is elsewhere/   for instance Chicago

Where is Bertold Brecht's last cigar?   I know it's dead
but where is it? hasn't anybody kept it/   intact?

What does President Kennedy's face look like when he's asleep?
What does the Pope look like?
I don't know the names of these faces and these sleeps

What does the name Anastoya Mikoyan mean?
            Jack? Michael maybe?
Is there a machine big enough to stitch circus tents
there must be/ or is it the Big Spider/   of Navaho?

Who made the flowery crusted cream-clotted tower
          of the Woolworth building?
Nostalgia made it
Who made Europe?   Nostalgia
Who made Africa?   Nostalgia
Who made America?
Nostalgia/

Nostalgia for what?   Try to remember
Doesn't anyone remember? Try   Try

THE MAN WHO SOLD MAHATMA GANDHI
LIFE INSURANCE

he was as you wd expect   an american
who had operated successfully out of Des Moines
                              Omaha & Tulsa
& who came 9500 miles to the City of Bombay
where he just happened to catch Gandhi
while he was having lunch

                    & sold him

a complete policy health security retirement coverage for life
& thereinafter redeemable   his beneficiaries. . .
all for the sum of. . .
at that time a rupee. . .
being worth a half dollar. . .

Homer P. Hogsbristle   what have you done?
        Ace salesman of the Mutual of Omaha

you have subverted the first saint of the Twentieth Century
a man whose lungs are directly inflamed
                              with the breathing of God
whose wife is folded   in the half-flexed knee-joint of God
whose children are on the eyelid of God

      "He sweet-talked me" Gandhi remarked in a news
interview some weeks later   when he had cancelled his insurance
      "If he'd come anytime earlier
I'd never have had all that money in my pocket.
If he'd come afterwards   I wouldn't have been interested"

Oh no   Guru
then

                    you'd have been fasting
                    you wd have been spinning
                    you wd have been way way way way out
                                    making salt

But consider this occult salesman
from Omaha   with his home-made product
how he came 9000 miles & sold it
to the least likely man on the whole earth
at exactly the right time

                              & if that isn't
a real act of american Black Magic I'll eat my hat

EYE AGAINST CONSOLIDATED EDISON

The smoke from Consolidated Edison   rises against the sky
Is it right to say that smoke   is part of my own life?
It unites all of us   It joins and unites
my hands & feet
legs
my nose eyeballs and throat   SMOKE
you have put me together out of a hundred pieces

No No   Word tricks!
I am naturally One Thing   It is words that divide   Lies
      lies
Body   I am speechless before you
Beautiful indescribable body in your entirety   I will say
      nothing about you
only   BREATHE!

Aaach   I have just breathed in a whole mouthful of soot
Like a true poet   I have thrown open the window
to communicate with you   Sky
and I am blackened under a whole bucketful of dry ash
                              from the stacks of Consolidated Edison

A mouthful of fresh air is worth a poem
A lungful of fresh air is worth a book of poems

BAKHUNIN

I come from Peter and Paul Prison. I am a fat man.
My sister visited me there.

Prison of thick stones where did you hide me?
Prison famous throughout the world for its large stones
did you hide me   deep
so that even the Neva   with its ships·
                        flowed over my head?
But I have torn loose like a tuft of moss
                        like an old spar   of rigging!

Riga   Pakov   Grodno   Lodz   Stettin   Lausanne
All you smoky stations
as I travelled across Europe in the opposite direction from Lenin
and much thinner

Open the locked doors!
Break open the sealed boxcar and let me out
like an old elephant
who has come to perform at a circus in small town
I still have my loose skin
            and enough bulk yet to raise tentpoles
I will amaze everyone   by my great feats of strength
                                    and compassion

O Change,   Brotherhood,
Intoxicating anarchism!
      Barricades bright with students and flags!
And you behind me   prison with the heavy stones
where my sister visited me   from our estate
remembering how I played to her on the balalaika
she   who had no interest in politics
came to bring me   wine
            and one or two delicacies I liked
wrapped in a white napkin

A WORKMAN'S DAY OFF

Jasper without tools   Jasper without his lunchbox and hot
     thermos
Jasper without shoes   Baggy pants decayed underwear
Jasper thrown up on his own sofa on sunday
like a shark beached on the sand.

An apartment is like a well, like the deepest of black wells.
At the bottom of this well lay Jasper's boy
                         playing with the cat.

Jasper: a hard fact
hands like bats   bakelite safety helmet
painted red by the Fuller Construction Co.
master plumber   his belt clinking with wrenches
thick skin   nails cracked in the cold
The New York skyline rises above him

No. It's sunday   The sky has fallen into the well
& there is no way of retrieving it.
The cat wreathes about the boy's feet.

Shape-changing cat: this cat has ten different shapes at least
square   curled   stretched and pulled out like taffee
coiled tight etc.   In the cold   the boy touches the cat's fur
as if it were the only thing left.

If a bucket could go down into the gloom
and pull those two up

Sunday afternoon   there is nothing for Jasper to do
except read the Daily News   Bruised he
watches the headlines of the world cascading over him
Hanoi Stanleyville Jackson, Mississippi
Madagascar DeGaulle bedridden
as the Atlantic Alliance crumbles

He sees none of these things
His arms ache
          unused
waiting for the weather of love to change

SKRUGG   THE FURNACE TENDER

Skrugg came into the plant when he was trained   and he
stayed there. There was another percussion under the
roof than the one he knew. It was different from the percussion
agitating the street   from the one agitating
his own blood

Sometimes the foreman stood behind him red in the face
and sometimes they shared a coffee thermos together
on the bending grid outside the forge.

The red eye of the forge flamed and flamed. Skrugg
watched it steadily with the same eyes as he watched the
shambling men on the streets   the men in his own
neighborhood that he knew were not working

Fuel slipped through the pipes—pale viscous fuel
diesel metered into the furnace by Skrugg. And when
it came it flamed and the beams ballasted inside the
furnace bloomed and bloomed

Pale amber colored diesel   bars passing from their white
climax to calibrations of rose   to rose-plum   to purple
Crane shuttling between the shop and the yard   crane
hoisting the hard plates with its magnet of charged ions
Skrugg watched the steel plates come into the plant and go
and the men come and go.

The plant had three eyes   the foreman's eye
the furnace's eye   and Skrugg's eye. Of these three
Skrugg's was the steadiest

Sometimes from the air   sometimes from the air over
the harbor   there came a curved lovely sound.
It fell like a whip through the window. It flaked off
the grey scales from the steel he had cooked
It hammered against his eyes   and softened Skrugg's
own backbone so that he almost had to cry to himself
Enough   enough

CITY HAIKU

1
Winter in the park
the seal sleeps in his seal skin
without buttons

2
A zoo walk; Old Kodiak and I
blowing steam at each other
between the bars

3
As the little boy bawls
he stuffs into his mouth
gumdrops

4
Sunday afternoon flower show:
Oops! My Aunt Harriet's boobies displayed
bending over gladioli

5
First city snow: the Puerto Rican janitor
throws down salt
with the gesture of sowing seed

6
Parks Commissioner Moses has died
leaving 5482 bird sanctuaries
without birds

COUNTRY HAIKU

1
Everywhere the grass
drinks up the night dew
as the little girl listens to stories

2
Barely a print on the dirt road
but some animal
has been eating choke-cherries

3
Terrified of everything
the summer visitors
have been hatching a caterpillar in an empty jam jar

4
Husband & wife
as alike as two beans
are making each other miserable

5
The first night camping out
Now the little boy's lugging home his sleeping bag
and some rags of trillium

6
Fra Angelica's colors: raw umber and green
        Going back to him / by way of the fields
this Spring day

FLEX

No pace like that of   Sumac unfolding
planes don't travel at such speed
wind and sky travel as fast as planes
light even faster

        wind/   sky/   and light
                            are the locale

       in which plane
                       is loosely buoyed

But the tight squeeze!
the combustion in the bud
     of sumac unfolding

Small galls and midges wintering in the fruit
don't know what it's about

     OLD SUMAC SPIRE
     rusty old red velvet   house
     that has survived winter
                   but won't survive the spring

     burst!
     and burgeoning
     of sumac unfolding

When the sheathe rips it sends out 2 or 3 extra feet
                  of leaf and stem in a few weeks!
the increase of sumac
the speed at which it accelerates

and the old stem still downy and soft
barely solidified from the liquid
of last year's spurt

     the flash
     and quick
     of sumac unfolding!

and the year's growth before that
not yet congealed into bark
skin still   rippled and scarred with

                         motion

showing which way the drive went
                              and stretched

          the flex of it!
          the quick spring
          and the unfolding!

See it
          with eyes on the inside
all you spiders/   midges/   and small bugs
          covered with the red velvet   dust
                    in the old WINTER PALACE

as the tree breaks
          and exceeds itself
unwinding at such a pace
          at such great speeds

MESSAGE

you ask me how they keep walking
                              the "Peace Walkers"
walking all the way from San Francisco etc
                    to Moscow
their message is too beautiful for me to encompass
                    in a poem

GOOD NEWS!

But as a mctaphor   let me point
to that long-legged   pregnant woman over there
in shorts and sneakers her bunched veins show
 like blue hyacinth spikes
& she wears a nice cool   peppermint striped blouse

In the sun she's walking heavily from one side of
                              this small playground to the other
And if she makes it
she will have taken as many steps/   as they
                    down/   the same road

19

JULY OPENING FOR PORTULACCA

Portulacca: Suddenly it's here!

not just in little dibs
at the flower border

                                        but the WHOLE RANGE
red   violet   pink   lime-green   orange
white
BLOOMS
&   it'll be like this the whole summer

Imagine/   never a single vibration
                    less than to-day

or growing in what the seed catalogue people
call "an unbelievable profusion"

                    And the same next year/   absolutely!

                    and the year after!

THE FOUR STAGES
                    for Franz Fanon: once a poet then doctor serving with
                                        the Algerian Liberation Army

Franz   I can't say   my life is not changed
Franz   correct me
            if these aren't the four stages of the journey
you made for both of us
1
A village buzzing with flies
the bus at Colombe-Bechar
        waits for the peasants with their baskets of chickens
We leave the dusty square
        journey by steamship from Algiers to Marseilles

the wonderful ride by night
        orchards of the french countryside lighted up
in the beam of the locomotive   train with its wheels
      its electrified switches   turbines
glides into Paris

                            .   Dawn
Franz   that trainride is worth
              40 000 years of African history

Village of Colombe-Bechar buzzing with flies
    the dry palm leaves clatter against each other
the children are throwing sticks
There is a massacre at Retif   which we don't hear about
450 algerians slaughtered by the gendarmes

At Oud-i-waka   at the quarries
the machine guns have cut down a hundred prisoners
but we don't think about it
          Only
about our escape!
We can't wait

                          as the bus   pulls out

          our hearts leap

2
In Paris we became human   ists
you with your black dick
I with my flint eyes   and bone knuckles
                    We became Greeks

Franz   you've had nothing to eat for three days
only the economies of John Stuart Mill
          and the theories of Leibneckt and Auguste Compte

the greenhouse of culture steams
Our voices have condensed
          in drops
      against the hot panes of glass
                of the Jardin des Plantes

WORDS!

Franz   what has happened to us?
   we've flipped out   dissolved into the european bloodstream
with your thick lips   pursed around the words
                as if you were eating peppers
you have schooled yourself to speak
                the pure couplets of Heredia

Franz!
   how many cups of coffee have we consumed
in the cafe   off Rue M. le Prince
drenched in the light of these silver candlebra?

But you are brought back to who you are
by the clatter of metal   a beggar at the curb
          rummaging thru the garbage can

You remember you are not white

3
This is the stage where you Play the Nigger
                                        like you say   Franz
as we in New York are making it with High Camp
up goes the priest's frock at mass
with a carrot up his ass
labelled "George Washington sucks"

we scandalize them in the name of the common humanity
                        POVERTY
                                is the only obscenity
I ask you:
Follow the child uphill
towards the barriada with its tin roofs
          La Paz Lima
she has filled her pail at the last city hydrant

and the boy walking down the road
with the dead rabbit under his coat (that Neruda describes)
          As the car of the rich man passes
          his eyes turn to two stones

In all of the rotten slums   Watts   Newark
                              Algiers
Dakar Brazzaville Johannesburg   Bogota   Capetown
the children beg for bread
the women are selling themselves
and the men have become pimps and police spies

Your brothers and sisters
        Franz   there is nothing else to do but dance and make fun

Franz   you have tossed away your scholarship
You have demolished your bowler hat
and kicked off your Italian leather shoes
ba- ruum   ba- ruum   ba- ruum
you dance barefoot in the dust
banging your ass as a drum
you have used the sun for an ear ring
& rattled your gold teeth

                        "Playing the Nigger"

4
So we have reached the 4th Stage
when the children on the road
                    are saying to you
        STOP MAKING POEMS

While we are dancing
                they have arrived to watch us: the sightseers
a busload of black realestate operators out of Dakar
they clap and throw pennies at our feet
                                Disgusting

Franz   Franz   who do you think you reach with your dusty
        dance
Franz   who do you want watching you?
        who do you want listening to you?

Think: the boy with the stone eyes
                            walking down the road
does he suddenly come to you   and light up?
does his face change?
And the whore waiting at the street corner
            her ear to the transistor radio
turned in to your music?   Is she purified?

In the forlorn suburbs of Africa shacks with the corrugated
                                            tin roofs
                    put together out of old crates
a moth loops by the streetlamp   in the hut
the whole family lies asleep on the mud floor
It's dark   and is it your song
                    that breaks thru the roof?

And the laborer who has worked all day for the white planter
he lies in the barracks on the wet pallet
                        his back scarred

Does your song heal the welts?

NO!   LIES!   LIES!

THEY ARE NOT LISTENING TO YOU

Franz
From the square at Colombe-Bechar comes the dry rattle of
                                            machine guns
Take it!
the Angel of Silence   stuffs his fist into your mouth

SONGS AND OTHER SONGS

In the barred wood   the Whitethroat
Sweet   sweet   sweet   pensive whistler   the Whitethroat
in my deep wood
in my barred wood

In the limed wood   the Flycatcher
the breezy whistler   and his sister the Veery   his sister the
        Veery
ee - o - lay   ee - o - lay   streaked liquid whistler
in my limed wood
in my limed pitchy wood

All birds sing songs of purest joy so it seems
the Flycatcher   the Veery   the honeyed Sparrow

                But of my own childrens' cries

which is the sweetest to me now
and which is the most bitter
in my barred wood
in my limed pitchy wood?

FOR KERSTIN

She has her hand in mine   Will she hate me then
when I'm old   and the leaves are cold
on the tree   and she and I
are no longer green?

Bits of wild newsprint are flying
the wind has blown my child against me in the street
She holds me with her blue mitten
Oh Kerstin   you know
this weather has put me
in one of my rare good moods

TIGERS

Wordless are her nightmares   Wordless
she wakes and looks up at me radiantly
my youngest child Liza
I bend over and brush

her hair dampened by sweat.   What animals came
with their tusks and eyes of staring red phosphorus
to pin you into the bed:

I break through the leaves and shake her gently
Her father stands half in vines
"The tigers have all gone. Would you like
a cup of water? I'll go down to the brown river
of Africa following their tracks"

MY FATHER-IN-ME

My father in me   walks down the street
a laughing ghost   in the snow.

                                    He is saying this to himself:
my son is the spitting image of me
now that he's fifty
he has the same loose-propelled gait and high stride
the same receding hairline
the same prognathic jaw   the same beefy complexion
the same careful cuffs
long effeminate hands thrust
into pockets stuffed with calendars and candy.

If he'd meet some forgotten cousin
on a night like this
                  (in the snow   in the wild snow)
he'd scare the hell out of her,
wearing my old wool toboggan cap

pulled down over his ears
as I pulled it down.
With his ragged eyebrows catching the snow
and his mustache rusted with cigar stumps
he has the same look I cultivated
whatever that was
with my own mustache   with my eyebrows.

                                        And he is saying:

This man is my apparition
he is the living replica of me if that's possible
he is my heiroglyph   writing me
on the walls and buildings as he goes by
 man with my shoulders and anklebones
with my shanks and knucklebones
man wearing my shoes
man with eyesockets
man with my skin and chin
man with my armpits
man with my paunch and abdomen
with my hips and haunches
with my cock

Man with my debonair air walking the dry night.
Only he is graver than me
he does not play the harmonica
and his eyes   where do they come from I wonder?

FATHER AND SON ON THE ROAD

The man who suddenly sang   in a deep voice
suddenly found himself singing in a deep voice
                in a full   unstopped voice
as they drove down the road   his son beside him
who always said Stop   Daddy don't sing
now said   Sing   Go on singing
and he sang in his new voice

                    in his new found profound basso voice
as the son was allowed to steer the car for the first time
the five year old boy   which he found he could do easily
                        holding onto the steering wheel with both hands
                                    at his father's knee
as his father sang loudly
then graduated to working the accelerator pedal
                                    with his feet
and shifting gears going uphill
            which he found he could do easily
            as his father sang deeply and profoundly
in his new voice
songs arias medleys which he had never been able to remember
                            or sing right
as the son steered and shifted gears   when necessary
and occasionally made minor repairs on the car
the son jumping out on the road
        to fix the pump the air intake the distributor
                    in a small way   while his father was singing
and to make a small clutch adjustment
while his father was singing   while his father was singing
                        deeply and meaningfully
ballads chanties snatches of popular operettas
hymns and school anthems
                            marches arias cantatas
        dolce et forte
tutte et maximum forte et vivace
in his new voice
while his son went on steering
                    and repairing the autombile
gradually mastering the whole thing
It came to the boy naturally
it was simply   normal growth
            open to every American   from birth
while his father went on singing
while his father went on miraculously and miraculously singing

AFTER THE DANCE *for my cousin Jeanne*

When she came home   her mother
        Mama   was she waiting up?

                                                    oh help!

It was like that
All night long deep into the first cock crow
Mama on her knees praying
to Our Lady of Linoleum:

            KEEP HER CLEAN
            DON'T LET THE BUGS LAND ON HER

In those days the slums were livelier
my grandfather   he owned a cherry tree

            Cherry tree   lean your branch
            softly   against the wire screening
            of the second-story window

Outside in the dark   cherries hang like black moons

LILLY'S SONG

She's left   Her touch is like my fine oak floor
all glow
When Lilly goes
she leaves my arms burning
No boat
        floundering   wallowing on a wave
aches for port
as I ache for her
She is my boat
all on fire with love fuel
She leaves
my walls   floor   windows   all burning/   spinning

WOODCHUCKS

Where have the birds gone
        this windy late afternoon?
Poking through in the meadow
            the new·shoots of green grass...
I will pay my respects to one or two woodchucks I know
They'll be wondering:
        what is this city man doing here
        out of season?

HUNTING WILDFLOWERS

That nice ramble through the woods
        when Mrs. Aschenbach showed Saxifrage and
                                Spring Beauty to me...
walking behind her blue pants
I remembered other flowers I'd·seen
both wild and cultivated

SHE IS

She is
arms around me   and the sea
pounds ' the river explodes its gulls
and the seaweed unwinds its
basketful of shells and small crabs
Was ever beach whiter than this
where she lies by my elbow
like the blown foam?

SOME LOVE POEMS

1
My love's body at noon
has closed with wine
her dark places are petals that have closed
she is a dreaming wood
I would not enter if I could

2
Driving north in spring rain
with nothing to think of:
except her whole body
        from the tips of her feet to   her hair
        loosened over my poor bed
The apple trees have come out!

3
What good to her are these poems
when I have to be away for three weeks?
even Catullus
telling how much he loved you
couldn't keep you green until he came again

4
What am I
that after just three weeks'
absence
the pressure of your mouth
turns me to water?

5
On the sidewalk
    the factory workers are already out

ah well, work to be done!

and my girl lies on my bed
    yawning
not even stretching her long legs

6
Loving you in the afternoon
is like burying my nose
in a great bush
        of cool newly-opened blue-violet tinted   lilacs
so deep
I can't even hear the birds

AFTER LABOR DAY

They have gone   not the sulphur-colored butterflies
but all the women and men swimmers
                                and river-soused kids

Under the ledge the pool lies cold after Labor Day
                                        its depths veiled
but the sulphur butterflies
                    their wings fragiler than rice paper
tumble in the sun

Wind   tear it loose   from the first stripped birch
                                    branch its yellow detritus
The wind tosses up the ribboning pale sulphur gusts
                                    of butterflies

they shred away   then coalesce again fitfully
and land on the hot sand at our feet

                                We lie on the sand watching them
our hair caught with leaves   your long tanned leg against mine
                wife

tied by what wry filaments
                after the separations of summer?

LOST COUNTRY

I have keys on my ring
                I have forgotten what they mean
I have a child in my house
                I don't know if she's mine
What is the color of the daisy's eye
in my lost country?

A city square in slush   somewhere near Boston?
Footprints there are slowly melting
slowly melting   footprints
      in the slush snow   melting
into the diagonal

between 8 black trees

A CANNUCK MATRIARCH

Sounds of the house   the principal sound
      my Grandmother Rose' sewing machine
                              (her name belied her temper)
      plunk in the middle of the front parlor

She was a small black widow
who spun out capes coats and collars
of seal   silver fox   mink   otter

      remember she said   I'm a fur worker
                              who's working for you
                              and don't you forget it

She emigrated from Canada
      my Grandmother Rose
      my brave Grandmother Rose
where in addition to the above there were
bear   lynx   wildcat   muskrat   wolves   reindeer
                              snowshoe rabbits   caribou

The blizzards of Canada filled the room
      I'll never forget   the sound of her needle
                              the chill of her Cold Code

as she labored for us piling up
tippets and ruffs   stoles   wraps and linings
                              for rich people
over our own poor sofa and chairs   window sill
                              lampshades   wardrobes and tables

THE DISHWASHER

Work   work   What the dishwasher feels
SCHLURRP   with his fish fingers
the day passes standing up

or Varya   in the Chekhov comedy who keeps saying
''We must work   work''
as the cherry orchards were cut down
The cherry blossoms grounded
minds revolted by their own idleness

The longing for work   the ache of unemployment
Lee shambling down 6th street
            Bimbo Rivas sings: ''a job
give me a simple job/   to meet the day
                  head on''

and man, what wouldn't I do with that paycheck.
They say a machine starts out with the equivalent
of a highschool education
            All of us standing around
day after day
unused

ON THE WING

As I roll past on the El
I wonder/   how can that house on the hill
                              stand?
Its floorboards are rotting
Its porch is falling apart
One of its wood turrets lean crazily towards me
It seems a cardboard house
a dollhouse for kids
Through the curtain blown aside suddenly
I see a woman combing her hair
& look!   on the roof   five Puertoriqueno   young men
      are letting loose & gathering in
                              pigeons

FOR KATYA   *the Pogrom*

It's not true   A woman can give until she has nothing left
Katya   I've had from you   apples
bread   & this book of Paul Goodman's poems
your head on my pillow   your leg
around mine   & from your lips   gossiping lore
about raising children — the miracle —
to be grown men and women!

A story about the death of your Uncle Grisha
A Cossack came riding across the stone streets of Tverdyansk
his lance was punched red
but the blood escaped. It comes   & still comes
into the veins   of your arms   so lovely
                        I do not dare touch them

Katya you live here on 11th   NYC   1960
But I know   this street is Tverdyansk
and this City has to accept your gift
of red flowers

SELF-PITYING POEM

When you hurt me
I walk away
I don't analyse
I play/   I ply my trade/
I have hammers & nails/   wrenches/   & screw drivers
                        I am employable
I have musical instruments
                        a harmonica   a banjo   an oboe
when one of them is broken I can go on playing
        tunes
I stay loose   I keep moving
When you hurt me   I walk away
I don't stop to locate the bruise

                                I'm black and blue all over
from other people beside you

THE DREAM *on my 50th birthday*

I dreamed I caught an owl   in an old coat
and it was my own heart

Hunter Hoo Hooo   Skree - eeek   Skyrider   Black
it dropped out of the dark
under the twigs of trees
into the underbrush at our knees
cut with the tracery of invisible black raspberries

I've caught an owl in the brambles!   under my dreamcoat
it billows out   out   My arms strain
            to hold down a whole field   of wings
heaving and fluttering trying to break out

Heart   when I wake
you'll never be the same again
I won't be able to keep you inside my ribs

CADMIUM RED COLOR

Fra Angelico   his eyes washed of the color of the Madonna
of her resplendent blue   came back to live in our town.
He embraced the poverty of our town   a poverty expressed
in the flaked stone and worn clapboards. The mill
was shut down and many of the houses empty.

Oh but the farming equipment out for sale! In the
dealer's yard all those new tractors   the bailers
spreaders and payloaders   the graders and all those
big fucking International Harvester trucks. They
gave back some of the glitter of the old town
as you drove by.

Fra Angelico had forgotten the gold aureoles. He wanted
all that heavy equipment painted cadmium red.
And it was painted that way.

FOG DRIFTING IN   *St. Valentine's Day 1859*

I am the Governor of the new State of Oregon
Over the black firs   fog drifts in from the Pacific
I have been here ten years   mixed gains & griefs
                              The greed
of these settlers.   Can I adjust claims?
               Loneliness
I have left home and friends behind —
        such as it was   such as they were —
                       for these "middling endeavors"
Many things occupy me now

No time to write poems

from **RAGAS FOR AHMA**

ALAP   *the invocation*

Ahma   I'm inside you.   I'm in deep.
And when we wake   you sit up   and shake me out of your hair
and prepare in the cold light
                       to return to the Frost King.
I have to say: Ahma   doesn't it matter who cares for you?
Doesn't love count?

Then it is that the pond in the park
fills with black leaves.
She has lost one of her earrings.
She looks at me with eyes that are not hers.

        *   *   *

A stillness. The sun has slipped from the window pane
Inside   the bed   the chair   a plain table
Inhabit the room with us.
The stove diminished beyond a doorway. And on the phonograph
Ali Akbar Khan   the sarod player
meditatively explores the scale of a late afternoon raga.

                    PP -i -i -i -i -i -i -nnnnnnnng !

his fingers open up the strings. And in between   SPACE:
a patch of blue sky across which clouds drift
as the drone   resonates over the canyon.
The musicians are looking at each other mostly waiting.
The tabla player hasn't come in yet.
Ahma lies with her legs stretched out at them
furious at me for not fucking her.

            *   *   *

Her step on the stair.   Will never come near
Still   I'm greedy for her just the same.
The bucket is being filled elsewhere   and in the kitchen
the plate scraped into the paper bag   as the cat
wreathes around the table leg. Domestic Felicity.
Well   that's shot to hell.   Here as elsewhere.

Still   I'm greedy for her. Memories. The scratch on the door:
I let her in.   And undress her down to the naked skin.
After that   dinner.   I devour her: every hour of the flux
the continuum.   "How *were* you today?"

                "I did such and such."

"Lovely Ahma   how gracefully you take all those hurdles.
And the children?"

                    "Oh   they're fine.   And well."
And mine?   Oh   fine   fine.

Her footfall on the stair
is a habit I shall never get rid of

            *   *   *

The Andaman Island Dead.   He's gone but he's not gone.
He's here   a presence above the ground
like the wind shimmering among the leaves   the mist rising

above the swamp.   The pale moon is an emanation of a
      former life
that reaches us in the vague signals among the fireflies
the banging of cooking utensils. The night spills and decays.
The old order.

He will speak to us as long as the bones still carry flesh.
As long as the body is covered with its frail shroud of
coconut cloth   fibers eaten by the moon.

Let him call the tune for a while
the dead man   rotting in our midst
with the power.

     *   *   *

I don't know what's happening in this city anymore
a shift   a weird screech in the cars shearing off different ways
The day slides   the sky's turquoise
veering to cobalt   to rose madder   under the mercury
      vapor lamps
                              Fire in the sky
                              Time going by

And on the other side of the river   what?   Summer maybe
                              After the ice break-up.
And on the other side of night   my woman changed
                              And brought back to me!

Smoke ravels from the stack high up over the Lehigh Freight
      terminal
Gloom under the expressway All the trucks have gone West
            Duluth   Oshkosh   Minneapolis
            vacancy in the metropolis

Night   night
Oh well.   Hello winter.   I've lost her.

     *   *   *

PAX
GIOIA

Reflections of Lucia Vernarelli (1920-1995)

Lucia was living with Ernst (Hacker) while we were at graduate planning school at Harvard. Around 1951. We were coming back from an evening concert of Bartok at Memorial Hall. Ernst said: "Bartok is my man." I first noticed Lucia in her red shoes.

In the Village in late '50s, Ernst & Lucia, Stanley Tankel & Clare and myself were friends. We had an occasional supper together. The three of us men were in a group (informal) on planning for Greenwich Village. Very advanced, idealistic. I remember being impressed by Ernst's somber discipline working for the N.Y.C. Planning Commission.

Grace (Paley) and I had dinner one evening at Ernst & Lucia's top-floor apartment on Fifth Avenue & 23rd Street. That's where I first appreciated her painting of a cat. Later we kept that cat in our kitchen.

Lucia—among many other talented women coralled by Grace because she loved me—did costumes/décor for a street play I had adapted: Everyman.

During antiwar years that group was very closely together—along with Carl—and draft counseling—& Lucia in basement of Washington Square Methodist Church. Around that time she and I talked books. I found out she was a reader. I was impressed when she lent me a 19th-century Sicilian novelist to read (study of early capitalism). By now I am a firm admirer of her paintings. But I know she produced not many.

We did *Address to the Smaller Animals* together. That was fun. She managed to unearth all her drawings and woodcuts. We would fit them into the book. She would put together a sequence and then undo it. I got to realize she would be always unable to decide.

A period of time. We helped her move from one apartment in Westbeth where there was too much street noise to another which was by an air duct vent. She didn't seem trivially or hypochondriacally oversensitive. Simply sensitive and superior cultivation to the bone.

Another period of time. I heard from friends she was not well in the head. I went to visit her in Westbeth. She took out all her paintings (at my urging). It was touching because they were mostly the same paintings. But she referred to them as being somehow tentative. A work "in progress," dating from perhaps yesterday or ten years ago. This lack of possession was heartrending because I always considered her a major painter. Even if she had been a major (recognized) painter she would have been an even finer . . . person. A person rare.

—Robert Nichols

Robert Nichols has been a poet, writer, landscape architect, and anti-war activist for many decades. In the 1960s Nichols co-founded the Judson Poets Theater off Washington Square, NYC. His books include *Slow Newsreel of Man Riding Train* (City Lights), *Daily Lives in Nghsi-Altai* (New Directions), *Address to the Smaller Animals* (for which this volume is the reprint), and *In the Air* (Johns Hopkins University Press). Robert Nichols makes no distinction between the literary and the political, as he and his wife (the late Grace Paley) were often quoted. This edition of *Address to the Smaller Animals* marks a long awaited triumph for readers, historians, and activists alike.